The *History* of Machines

by Judith McKinnon

Rigby

Contents

Machines Around Us

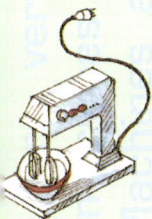

Machines are everywhere. When we ride in a car, watch a video, or use a computer, we are using machines. These machines are very modern, but humans have used simple machines such as pulleys for thousands of years.

Pulleys

Lifting heavy things can be hard work. In ancient times, people threw a rope over a tree branch to make it easier to lift a load. Then, in ancient Assyria, someone invented the pulley. The pulley is a simple machine that helps people lift heavy objects.

modern pulley

Today, cranes use large pulleys to lift heavy objects. A crane operator controls the crane from inside the cab. Without cranes, it would be very hard to build tall buildings.

Levers

When you sit on a seesaw or use a bottle opener, you are using a lever.

Levers help us move things. Early in history, people discovered they could use levers to move heavy objects, such as large rocks.

Archimedes, a scientist in ancient Greece, said he could even move the earth with a lever, if only he had a place to stand!

Pianos use many levers. When you hit a piano key, a lever inside the piano lifts a small hammer that hits a string. The string makes the sound. Each piano key has its own lever.

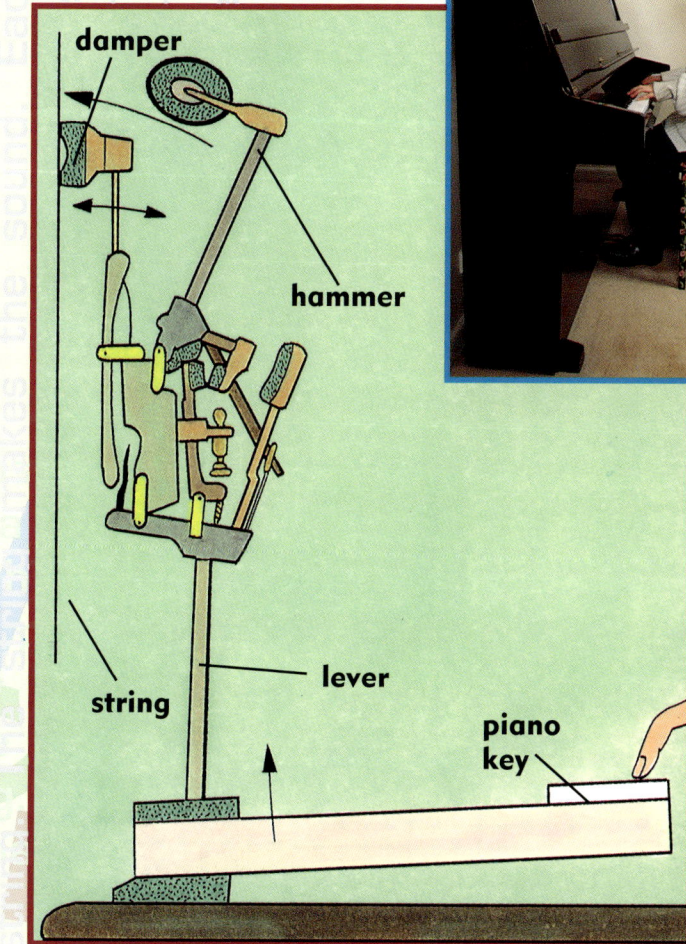

damper

hammer

string

lever

piano key

Wedges

People have used wedges as knives and axes for thousands of years. The first cutting tools were made by chipping pieces of rock into wedges.

Wedges have one thin end and one thick end. This makes them good cutting machines. The edge of every blade is a wedge.

Wedges are also very useful digging machines. Early farmers made a simple digging tool from a wedge-shaped stick.

Later, the **plow** was invented. Plows were often pulled by oxen or horses. Today, plows are pulled by tractors, but they still use a simple wedge to break the soil.

early digging tool

early plow pulled by oxen

horse-drawn plow

tractor pulling a modern plow

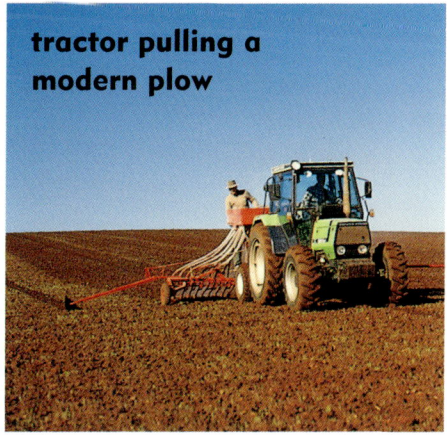

Ramps

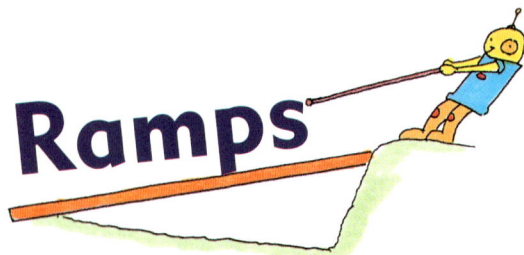

Ramps make it easier to go up and down a slope. For thousands of years, people have used small ramps for jobs such as loading animals into a cart. Ramps were often made from wood or packed earth.

Long ago, people made staircases by adding steps to ramps. Today, the escalator is a moving ramp with stairs. Escalators can move many people at one time. This is important in busy places like airports and shopping centers.

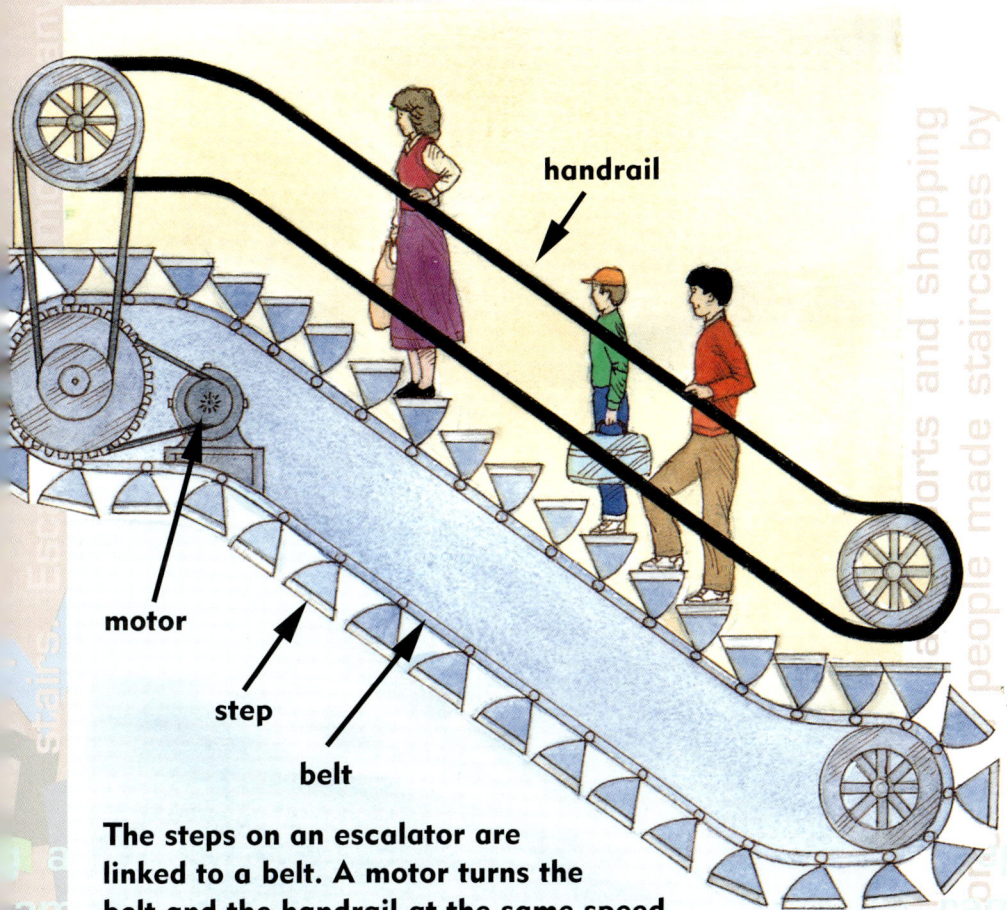

handrail

motor

step

belt

The steps on an escalator are linked to a belt. A motor turns the belt and the handrail at the same speed.

Wheels for Transportation

The wheel has been a useful machine since it was invented about 5,000 years ago. Wheels were first used to spin pottery, but soon people put wooden wheels on carts to make travel easier.

A little over 100 years ago, the first car was built. It had wheels with metal rims, which made the ride very bumpy. Later cars used **pneumatic** tires filled with air.

Reels Are Wheels

Movie cameras were first used at the end of the 1800s. They had wheels called **reels** that fed the film past a camera **lens**. As the film rolled across the lens hole, it recorded the action.

Today, we watch lots of movies on videocassette recorders. Videocassettes have reels, or spools, inside them. You can see them if you look closely at the cassette. The film runs from one reel to the other as the movie is played.

This videocassette has been opened to show the spools inside.

Wheels with Teeth

Gears are wheels that have teeth around their outside edges. Many years ago, people used windmills to grind grain into flour. The windmills used gears to turn the **millstone,** which ground the grain.

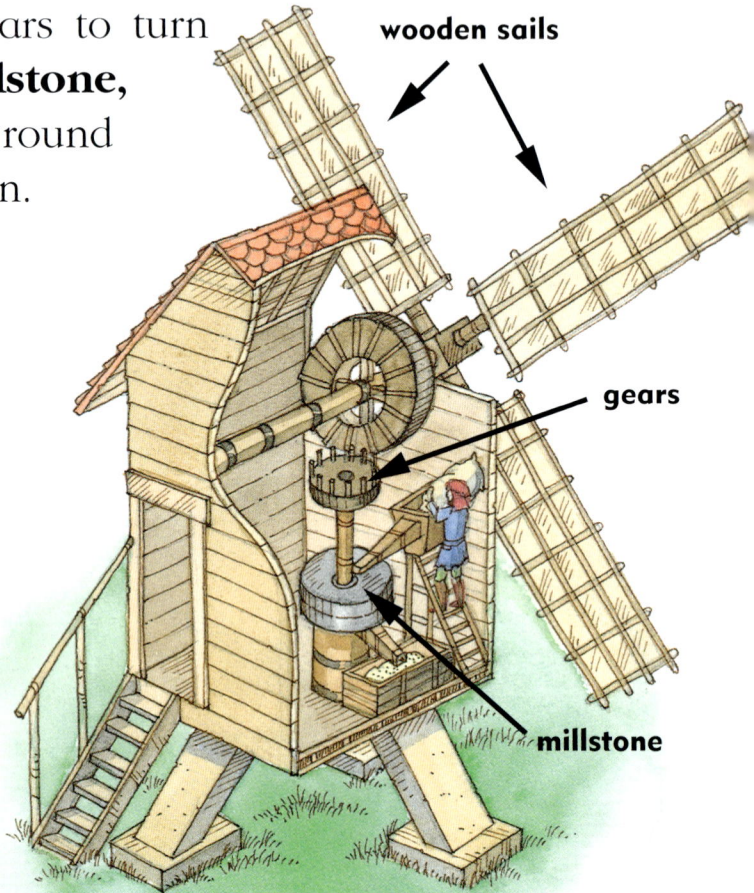

wooden sails

gears

millstone

Later, people discovered that they could use gears to make clocks and watches. The first clocks were wound up with a key. Windup toys and music boxes also use gears to make them work.

A watch has many tiny gears inside it.

Machines That Work Together

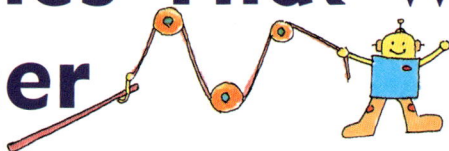

Over the years, inventors have discovered ways to put simple machines together to make new machines.

The invention of the bicycle gave people a new way to travel using wheels. Adding gears made it easier to pedal uphill. Brake levers made bicycles easier to stop.

brake lever

gears

gear
levers

wheel

19

Lawn mowers also use many simple machines. They use blades (which are very thin wedges), and they move on wheels. In some lawn mowers, gears help the wheels move more easily.

each blade
is a wedge

wheel

Machines and the Future

How do you think machines will change our future? Perhaps robots will clean our houses. Maybe we will ride in rocket-powered cars. We might even have **Internet** classrooms instead of going to a school!

Whatever happens, one thing is certain. As long as people have new ideas, there will always be new machines. *You* might even invent a machine of your own some day!

Glossary

gears   a system of wheels that have teeth around them. The teeth mesh together, helping a machine to do work.

Internet   an international computer link that allows people to communicate using computers.

lens   a curved piece of glass used in cameras to capture light.

machine   a mechanical invention that makes it easier to do work.

millstones   large, flat stones that are used to grind grain into flour.

plow   a digging machine that is used to prepare a field for planting crops.

pneumatic   filled with air under pressure.

reel   a wheel that winds on rope, film or other flexible materials.